AMAZING
Islands

100+ Places That Will Boggle Your Mind

SABRINA WEISS & KERRY HYNDMAN

What on Earth Books

CONTENTS

A note from the author

The view from the window of a plane when descending onto an island is a spectacular sight. And I've been lucky enough to see it more than once! The changing colors of the ocean never cease to amaze me. As a wildlife enthusiast and certified diver, I have traveled to many islands, from Sri Lanka to Indonesia and Cuba, so naturally I was excited to share my experience of them in this book.

The islands that fascinate me the most are the ones that remain virtually untouched by humans. For my research, I sifted through books and academic papers and made some incredible discoveries. There are so many amazing islands out there! I printed out a world map so that I could plot everything from my long list—the idea was to cover all of the oceans and have a mix of countries and landscapes. This process reminded me of the way that I would spin a globe that I had as a child and keep pointing my finger at a country until I came across one I didn't know. While working on the world map for *Amazing Islands*, I realized that some of the most interesting places were too small to see, so I had to look at a virtual globe instead. By using Google Earth, I was able to zoom into the middle of the oceans and look for islands that I never would have been able to find otherwise.

I knew that I wouldn't be able to set a foot on these particularly remote islands any time soon, so reading about them and retelling their stories transported me there. My hope is that readers will experience the same. It is the not so obvious stories of island life that made it into this book. With thousands to choose from and only so much space available, I picked stories that will stick with readers for a long time and inspire their own island adventures.

Acknowledgements

Sabrina Weiss
To Papi, my father. You took me on my very first island adventures. Building sandcastles on the beaches of the Canary Islands, finding our way through the intricate waterways and narrow streets of Venice, and plunging deep beneath the waves in the Maldives. I can still see these images before my eyes.

Kerry Hyndman
For Ivy & Mike, with thanks for all their help and support.

WHAT IS AN ISLAND?

An island is a piece of land that is completely surrounded by water. The size, shape, and location of islands make each one unique. Some are tiny, and others are vast. Some are made of sand and others are made of rock. Still others are covered in lush rainforest. The largest island in the world is Greenland at 836,297 miles² (2,166,000 km²). Many of the animals and plants living on islands are not found anywhere else on Earth.

A home for humans

Islands are home to more than 700 million people. That's about a tenth of the world's population. If you live on an island, anything that can't be made on the island has to be brought across water. So island people have learned to make the most of what they have. Many indigenous island people have diets, languages, and customs that are specific to their homes.

The island mass effect

Islands cause the water surrounding them to move in different ways to the rest of the ocean. This brings cold water, from deep in the ocean, up to the surface. And with it come huge amounts of food that a lot of creatures depend on. That's why we often find colorful coral reefs teeming with life in the shallow waters around islands.

Rhinoceros hornbill

Borneo

The many names of islands
• Islet, skerry, or cay — these are names for very small islands.
• Ait — a small island, often found in a river or lake.
• Archipelago — a group of islands. The Galápagos Islands and the Philippines are two examples.
• Coral island — an island in tropical waters that is made of coral. Rock and sand also help build up these islands.
• Atoll — a coral reef that has grown in a ring. They form around a volcanic island, which has sunk under the water.

Bajau
The Bajau people are also known as "Sea Nomads." They build houses on stilts in the ocean near islands in the Philippines, Indonesia, and Malaysia. Some Bajau divers spend so much time under water that their eyes adjust to see best there. And some can even hold their breath for up to 13 minutes!

HOW ARE ISLANDS MADE?

Most of the world's islands are created naturally. Some are formed by erosion—when water or wind move sand or dirt around. Others are formed by pieces of the Earth's crust moving away from or past one another. And others are created by the eruption of volcanoes. The oldest islands are millions of years old, but others are still just babies. Here are a few of the ways that islands are created by our amazing planet.

Padre Island

BARRIER ISLANDS

A barrier island is a long, narrow, sandy stretch of land that runs next to a coastline. It is separated from the mainland by shallow water. This type of island is formed of sand that has been moved to and left near a coast by the movement of the sea. They are called barrier islands because they protect coasts from the full force of powerful storms. Padre Island in Texas is the longest in the world at nearly 124 miles (200 km).

Mont Saint-Michel
This abbey on this island is home to an order of Benedictine monks.

WEATHER AND WAVES

Some islands are created by erosion. Weather and water wear away at the land until an island is isolated from the mainland. Tidal islands are formed in this way. However, they only really become islands when the tide is high. When this happens, water covers the piece of land that connects the island to the mainland. Mont Saint-Michel in France is an example of a tidal island.

VOLCANIC ISLANDS

Oceanic islands lie far out in the open ocean and were created by underwater volcanoes. As these volcanoes erupted, they built up layers of lava that finally rose above the water, forming land. Roca Partida is a volcanic island. It may be small, but it is busy. The nutrients that rise up from the deep sea around this island attract lots of marine life. Birds called Nazca boobies also nest there.

Roca Partida

Nazca booby

Hammerhead shark

Bottlenose dolphin

Comb jellyfish

Giant manta ray

CONTINENTAL ISLANDS

There are two ways that continental islands form. The first happens when continents break up. Around 299 million years ago, there was a single massive continent called Pangaea. This supercontinent broke apart as the Earth's crust moved. Fragments of land moved away and became islands. Madagascar (see page 14) is a continental island that was formed in this way.

Continental islands also form when seas rise. About 18,000 years ago, the Earth was covered in large ice sheets, called glaciers. As the planet warmed up, these glaciers started to melt, and sea levels rose. The rising water flooded low-lying land and created islands. The British Isles (see page 36) formed this way.

ISLANDS IN PERIL

Islands face many environmental threats, from climate change and rising sea levels to deforestation and overfishing. Sadly, it is common to see beaches awash with plastic and other waste. When people toss plastic into rivers and the ocean, it can travel along ocean currents and end up on remote islands.

SOUTH GEORGIA
British Overseas Territory

Human activities can have bad effects on remote islands. Cruise ships bring tourists to places like South Georgia, in the southern Atlantic Ocean. Visitors must follow rules to make sure they do not hurt the environment. They are advised to take nothing but pictures and leave nothing but footprints.

Elephant seal

South Georgia pipit

Beware of invaders

Islands tend to have lots of endemic species. This means that the island creatures will not have encountered most of the other animals that live on Earth. When humans travel to an island, they sometimes bring animals with them. They may do this on purpose. For example, they might bring goats or pigs to eat. However, this can also happen by accident—rats and other small pests often stow away on ships. The invaders can bring disease, compete with native plants and animals for food, or prey on native species. In some places, the new species have even completely wiped out native ones.

Rising sea levels

Our planet is warming up. Higher temperatures cause glaciers and ice sheets to melt and water to flow into the ocean. The result? Sea levels start to rise. Because of their small size and low elevation, islands and other low-lying areas are the first to feel the pressure. Many islands are at risk from flooding or, even worse, being completely submerged. Islands are good indicators of changes in sea levels—it is easier to monitor sea level here than on the mainland.

Tourist trouble

It's no wonder that tourists want to experience the beauty of the world's islands. But their visits can cause many problems. Islands can quickly become overcrowded, and the land and seas can get polluted with trash. However, in some places tourists take good care of the island. This approach is called sustainable tourism. Sustainable tourism can bring much-needed money to island communities. It can also help fund conservation projects to protect an island's natural beauty.

GALÁPAGOS

Ecuador

The Galápagos is an archipelago. It is made up of rocks, volcanic islands, and more than a hundred islets. They cover an area of 16,988 miles² (44,000 km²). That makes the Galápagos about the same size as Switzerland.

The Galápagos Islands were formed by erupting volcanoes. Layer by layer, lava built up and hardened into rock. Española, the oldest island in the Galápagos, is about four million years old. But the islands of Fernandina and Isabela are young. They are only about one million years old and are still growing! Around 9,000 animal and plant species live in the Galápagos. Among them are the only penguins in the northern hemisphere, marine iguanas, and flightless cormorants.

Island mail

The first "post office" on the islands was put up in the 1700s. Letters were left in a wooden barrel for sailors on passing ships to pick up and deliver. Today, tourists drop off postcards for family and friends. While they're there, they might pick up another addressed to a place that they are traveling to. They can then mail or hand-deliver the letter.

Darwin's finch
(also called Galápagos finch)

Prickly pear cactus

Lonesome George
This giant tortoise from the Galápagos island of Pinta was the last of his kind. He lived to be about 100 years old.

Galápagos penguins

DARWIN'S FINCHES

In 1835, Charles Darwin observed some interesting species of finch on the Galápagos. Each finch had the perfect beak to eat certain foods on the island where it lived. Darwin discovered that all of the finches began as a single species. Over time, they evolved into 14 species with differently sized and shaped beaks. This discovery led to Darwin developing his famous theory of natural selection.

1.

2.

3.

4.

Darwin illustrated four species of finch for his book
On the Origin of Species, published in 1859.
1. and **2.** have broad beaks for crushing seeds;
3. has a smaller beak for eating seeds from the ground;
and **4.** has a longer beak for capturing insects.

Fancy feet

Boobies are seabirds with brightly colored feet. The red-footed variety are found nesting throughout the Galápagos in trees and shrubs. Their cousins, the blue-footed boobies, show off their flashy blue feet in a dance to attract a mate.

Red-footed booby

Marine iguana

Flightless cormorant

ANIMALS TAKE OVER

Some remote islands have become overrun by one species of animal. One island is covered with meowing cats. Another is home to millions of snapping crabs. The lack of predators means these animals can multiply, making the island their own personal territory. Here are a few of the islands where a single species of animal reigns supreme.

KOMODO ISLAND
Indonesia

The largest lizards in the world, Komodo dragons are native to this island. They grow to 10 feet (3 m) long and weigh around 331 pounds (150 kg). That's more than a giant panda! They will eat almost anything they can catch, from small rodents to hefty water buffalo. They also eat their own species, and will munch down newly-hatched dragons without a second thought. Dragons launch surprise attacks on large prey, slashing them with their claws and shark-like teeth.

DANGER ISLANDS
Antarctica

Scientists wondered what was going on when they saw great patches of poop on these islands in pictures taken from space. It turned out that around 1.5 million Adélie penguins are crammed onto the rocky archipelago off the tip of the Antarctic continent. For most of the year, the area is covered by heavy sea ice, so hardly any ships come past. No wonder this colony managed to hide in plain sight for thousands of years.

SHEDAO
China

This tiny island covers an area of 0.28 miles² (0.73 km²). That's about the size of 78 soccer fields. Shedao is home to a huge population of venomous pit vipers. Scientists estimate that there are around 20,000 of them! These snakes are not found anywhere else in the world. They lie in wait on tree branches until their favorite winged food arrives. They like to eat small birds like the Chinese egret or black-tailed gull that stop over on the island during their spring and autumn migrations.

AOSHIMA
Japan
About 130 cats prowl this sleepy fishing village. Incredibly, they outnumber humans ten to one! The felines were first brought in to help control the rat population, but they quickly multiplied. Today, the island is also overrun by tourists who want to visit the cats, snap photos, and give them food.

CHRISTMAS ISLAND
Australia
During the rainy season on this island, tens of millions of bright red crabs march from the rainforest to the coast. There they breed and drop their eggs in the ocean. The crabs' eggs hatch as soon as they come in contact with seawater. The zoea (zoe-ee-uh), or newly-hatched larvae, live in the sea for a month before changing into tiny 0.2-inch- (5-mm-) long crabs and crawling onto the beach.

MADAGASCAR

Madagascar is the fourth largest island in the world. Humans didn't settle there until some 2,000 years ago. Lots of people live on Madagascar now, though—more than 25.5 million. But the island has an even larger number of animal residents.

About 90 per cent of all the animals and plants on Madagascar are endemic. This means that they are not found anywhere else on Earth. Madagascar used to be part of an ancient supercontinent called Gondwana. Then Earth's moving crust split the continent into separate landmasses. For the 88 million years since the split, animals and plants on the island have evolved in complete isolation.

Indri

Aye-aye

Aye-aye
This long-fingered lemur has rodent-like teeth that are always growing. It uses its thin middle finger to tap on trees and find grubs to eat.

Ring-tailed lemur

Leaf-tailed geckos are hard to spot among the trees.

Leaf-tailed gecko

Leaping lemurs
Lemurs are only found in Madagascar, but they come in many colors and sizes. The indri is one of the largest at 28 inches (72 cm). Mouse lemurs are the smallest, measuring just four inches (11 cm) excluding the tail. Lemurs use their long tails to balance when jumping from branch to branch.

Madame Berthe's mouse lemur

Panther chameleon

Palm oil crisis

Indonesia is the biggest producer of palm oil in the world. It provides a great income to the country, but it comes at a cost. Palm oil is used in many everyday products, such as cooking oil and chocolate, ice cream and soap. The problem is that there is now such a high demand for this oil that forest areas are destroyed so that people can grow more oil palms. Orangutans are suffering from this deforestation. Once the trees are gone, the apes have no home. Many organizations are trying to stop deforestation and save orangutans from extinction.

Roaming tigers

Sumatran tigers have a deep orange coat and contrasting black stripes. Sadly, they are hunted for their valuable fur and bones. Fewer than 400 remain in the wild.

SUMATRA

Indonesia

Like Madagascar, the dense rainforests of Indonesia have incredible wildlife and plants. Sumatra is one of the largest islands of this Asian country. Its most iconic residents are tigers, orangutans, rhinos, and elephants.

Since it is right at the equator, Sumatra's climate is tropical all year round. One minute the weather is hot and humid. The next, it's pouring with rain. The highlands are slightly cooler and less humid. These are better conditions for people to grow crops, such as coffee, vegetables, and rice.

RECLAIMED BY NATURE

Humans have tried to settle in all parts of the world. Mostly they have been successful. However, some islands are so off-the-grid, freezing cold, or lacking in food and fresh water that people abandoned them in search of more hospitable places. When people leave, nature is left to thrive, often with astonishing results.

FANGATAUFA AND MURUROA
France

In 1962, the French government built a nuclear testing site on these atolls in the Pacific Ocean. Over the next 30 years, roughly 200 nuclear bombs were blown up there. Some sea creatures were killed off, and dangerous radiation kept people away. However, life in the ocean is returning. The chambered nautilus and other sea mollusks have started to recover since the tests stopped.

DECEPTION ISLAND
Antarctica

Many people, from whale hunters to scientists, have tried to settle this horseshoe-shaped island. Some stayed for almost 20 years. Then, in the 1960s, volcanic activity finally forced people off Deception Island. In the summer, a few scientists and tourists visit. During winter, all that's left are decaying buildings, whale skeletons, and a colony of chinstrap penguins.

HASHIMA ISLAND
Japan

Over 5,000 coal miners and their families lived on Hashima Island until the mines were closed in 1974. The rocky island is no more than 1,575 feet (480 m) long by 525 feet (160 m) wide. It used to be one of the most densely populated places on Earth. Since the miners left, the concrete high-rise buildings have been crumbling, and plants grow along their collapsed walls.

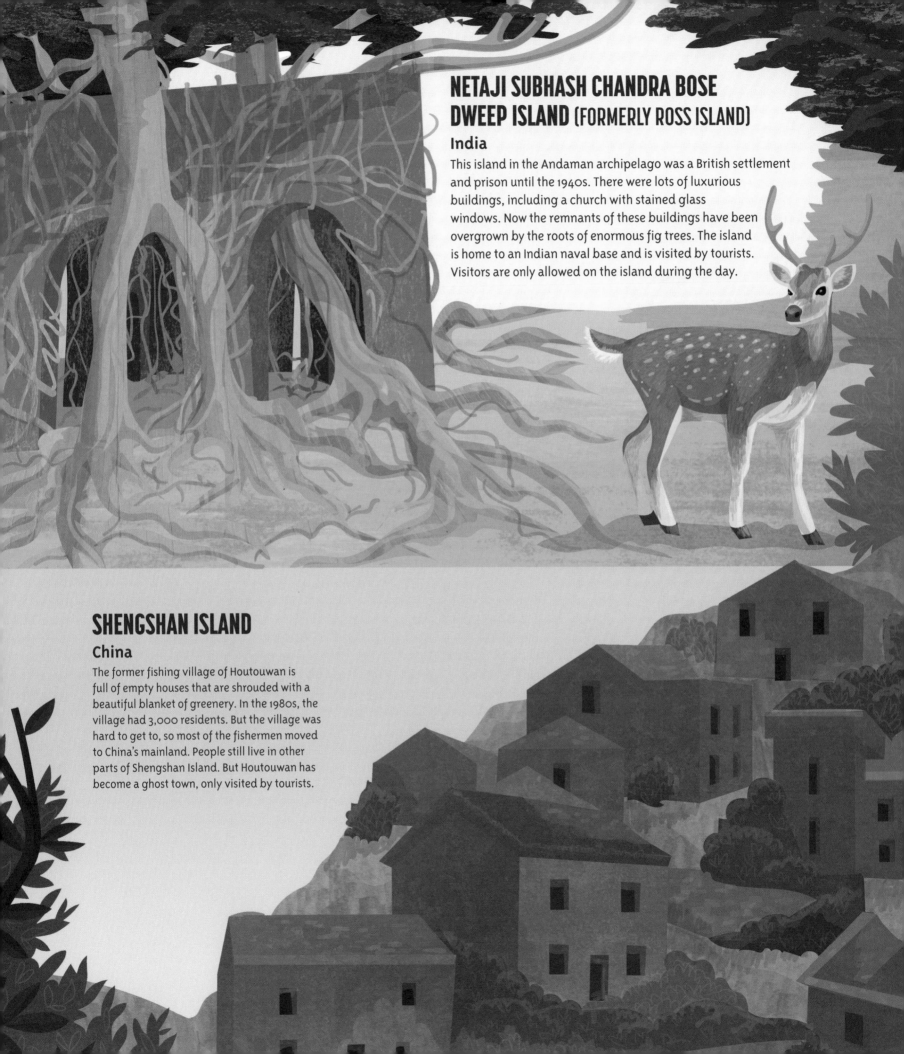

NETAJI SUBHASH CHANDRA BOSE DWEEP ISLAND (FORMERLY ROSS ISLAND)

India

This island in the Andaman archipelago was a British settlement and prison until the 1940s. There were lots of luxurious buildings, including a church with stained glass windows. Now the remnants of these buildings have been overgrown by the roots of enormous fig trees. The island is home to an Indian naval base and is visited by tourists. Visitors are only allowed on the island during the day.

SHENGSHAN ISLAND

China

The former fishing village of Houtouwan is full of empty houses that are shrouded with a beautiful blanket of greenery. In the 1980s, the village had 3,000 residents. But the village was hard to get to, so most of the fishermen moved to China's mainland. People still live in other parts of Shengshan Island. But Houtouwan has become a ghost town, only visited by tourists.

An army of white coats

Cuba is well known and admired for its healthcare system. The country has one of the highest numbers of doctors and nurses in the world in proportion to its population. In fact, many of them travel to other countries to help in times of need. There are about 50,000 Cuban doctors helping patients in 67 countries around the world.

CUBA

The island of Cuba is an independent country in the Caribbean Sea. It has a communist government, which means that everything is shared equally and there is little private ownership. It also means that education and healthcare are free for all. Because it is communist, some other countries won't trade with it. So Cubans have become very self-sufficient. They grow a lot of what they eat themselves and repair machines instead of replacing them.

Dancing in the street

On many Cuban streets, musicians play salsa music on guitars, bongos, and maracas. Couples dance to the music with lively, fast movements.

Cuban cars

Colorful old cars roam the cities, most of them as taxis. From 1959 to 2011, it was against the law to bring cars or car parts from other countries to Cuba. Cubans had to use spare parts to fix their vehicles.

Dominoes

One of the nation's favorite pastimes is playing dominoes in parks or out on the street. The Cubans play by their own rules, usually in teams of two seated around a wooden table.

PRISON ISLANDS

Over the centuries, countries around the world have used islands as prisons. Being surrounded by water made them harder to escape from than prisons on the mainland, but that didn't stop prisoners from trying. Most prison islands are no longer used. Some have even become tourist attractions.

COIBA

Panama

Coiba Island was used as a prison for almost 100 years before it closed in 2005. It has remained virtually untouched ever since, and plants have grown through the prison's abandoned ruins. The surrounding coral reefs are teeming with wildlife. More than 800 different species of fish, shark, whale, dolphin, and turtle live here. Some of the world's rarest birds can be seen on the island, including the scarlet macaw, Coiba rusty-backed spinetail, and crested eagle.

ÎLE SAINTE-MARGUERITE

France

Île Sainte-Marguerite is covered with fragrant pine and eucalyptus forests and is edged with rocky coves. The main attraction is Fort Royal, a former prison which housed "the Man in the Iron Mask" in the 17th century. This prisoner's identity is a mystery because he hid his face with a mask, which was actually made of velvet. Some people think he could have been imprisoned for a political scandal or even be a scorned relative of French king Louis XIV.

ALCATRAZ
United States of America

Located in San Francisco Bay, Alcatraz was a working prison between 1934 and 1963. It housed some of America's most ruthless criminals, including gangster Al Capone and train-robbing bandit Roy Gardner. Known as "The King of the Escape Artists," Gardner once jumped from a moving train to escape capture. There were 14 escape attempts made by 36 prisoners in Alcatraz. Officially, none were successful, however, five of the prisoners did vanish. It is assumed that they drowned. Today, tourists can visit the island and stroll through the cells and gardens.

ROBBEN ISLAND
South Africa

South African human rights activist Nelson Mandela was held here for 30 years, along with many other people who opposed South Africa's apartheid regime. Under apartheid, the government forced people of different races to live separately and discriminated against people of color. In 1994 Mandela was released from prison and went on to become president of South Africa. Robben Island is no longer a prison. It is now home to many animals, including endangered African penguins.

SPINALONGA
Greece

In the past, some islands have been used to isolate people suffering from diseases. In 1903, many Greek people with leprosy, a disease that affects the nerves and skin, were sent to live on the island of Spinalonga. At the time, people were worried that the disease was contagious, and the patients were forced to live in harsh conditions with little medical support. In 1957, those who had not already been cured were moved to proper hospitals. Black flags were placed on the island in 2012 to serve as a reminder of its sad history.

PHILIPPINES

The Philippines is part of the Malay Archipelago—the largest group of islands in the world. There are more than 7,600 islands that make up the Philippines. People live on only 2,000 of them. Most of the others don't even have names.

1 LUZON

The largest and most populated island in the Philippines, Luzon is home to Manila, the country's capital city. The island has many rice terraces. These are stepped fields carved into the mountains that are used to grow rice. They were created more than 2,000 years ago by the Ifugao people.

2 TAAL VOLCANO

Within Luzon island there is another amazing island. Taal volcano has a lake inside it and within that lake is a small island!

3 CORON

Several shipwrecks lie in the waters around this island. The Japanese ships were hit by American airstrikes during the Second World War.

4 CEBU

Every January, the grand Sinulog Festival is held here in honor of baby Jesus. It's a massive street parade with people wearing colorful costumes and dancing the traditional Sinulog dance to the sound of drums.

5 PALAWAN

A five-mile– (8.2-km-) long river flows underground through caves and mineral formations on this island.

6 SIQUIJOR

Siquijor was nicknamed "Island of Fire" by Spanish explorers who sailed past it at nighttime in the 16th century. They observed an eerie glow of swarms of fireflies among the molave trees under the night sky.

7 BOHOL

The Philippine tarsier is a small primate found on this island. Its body is so tiny (six inches [16 cm]) that its eyes and ears appear giant. In fact, it has the largest eyes of any mammal in relation to the size of its body. This shy animal hunts at night and loves to feast on insects, spiders, small lizards, and birds.

8 SIARGAO

The surfer capital of the Philippines, Siargao is famous for its Cloud 9 wave. Sometimes, surfers will wait for days until strong offshore winds create a wave with a hollow tube that they can ride through.

ISLAND PEOPLES

The earliest inhabitants of a place are called the indigenous people. As other people arrive later, they add their cultures to the mix. Lots of islands have a rich heritage that is created by this mixing of cultures. And on some islands, indigenous peoples have preserved all or some of their traditional ways of life, which often date back thousands of years. Here are a few indigenous island cultures.

NORTH SENTINEL ISLAND
India

In the Bay of Bengal lives a hunter-gatherer tribe that is completely isolated from modern civilization. Very little is known about the Sentinelese people, and no one outside the island speaks their language. The tribe has had almost no contact with the outside world and fiercely protects its island. Outsiders who try to make contact are chased away by a flurry of arrows.

NEW GUINEA

The island of New Guinea is divided into two parts— the Indonesian provinces of Papua and West Papua and the country of Papua New Guinea. There is a great diversity on the island. Nearly 850 different languages are spoken here! Every year, thousands of indigenous people assemble in a small town called Goroka. They wear their traditional dress, including feathered headdresses and colorfully painted faces, and perform their cultural songs and dances.

TENERIFE
Spain

People on Tenerife love a fiesta: whether it's celebrating the harvest festival in traditional dress, jumping over fire, or bathing goats in seawater during their midsummer festival. The goat bathing happens during the summer solstice, the longest day of the year. It has its roots in ancient traditions of the native Guanche people. The Guanche believed that the sea at midsummer possessed powerful qualities and bathing in it brought good luck.

HAINAN
China

The earliest settlers of Hainan, the Li people, were superb singers and musicians. Their folk songs are still sung today and are accompanied by traditional instruments. There are bamboo flutes played with the nose, mouth harps, and wooden drums. Li women are also particularly skilled in spinning and weaving cotton and silk to make clothes and other textiles.

NEW ZEALAND

The Māori are the indigenous inhabitants of New Zealand. They arrived from Southeast Asia around 1,000 years ago. One of their traditional arts is weaving sedge (a grasslike plant) into mats, hats, and baskets. Some Māori also perform an ancient dance called the Haka. In it, dancers thump their chests, stomp their feet, and stick out their tongues to prepare for battle or greet visitors. The All Blacks rugby team performs this ceremonial dance today, to challenge their opponents before a game.

EASTER ISLAND
Chile

This island in the Pacific is known for the incredibly large, ancient stone heads that can be found there. The heads are called Moai and were carved by indigenous people between the 10th and 16th centuries. There are nearly 1,000 Moai made from solidified volcanic ash and no two are the same. No one knows how or why these heavy, giant statues were transported to their locations. Some believe they may have pointed the way to drinkable groundwater.

HONG KONG

Special Administrative Region of China

More than seven million people live in this metropolis. Hong Kong can be divided into three parts: Kowloon on the mainland, Hong Kong Island, and the New Territories, which include more than 200 outlying islands.

Hong Kong Island has the most skyscrapers of any island in the world. There is little space to spread out, so the city has been built upward with high-rising houses and offices. The tallest building is a commercial center and hotel standing at 1,588 feet (484 m) tall and with an exhausting 108 floors. However, the most famous skyscraper is Central Plaza on Hong Kong Island. At its summit are lights that change color every 15 minutes to indicate the time.

Lantau Island

Sitting atop Lantau Island is a giant bronze statue of Buddha. It is truly enormous at 112 feet (34 m) tall and 275 tons (250 metric tonnes) in weight. Tourists can take a cable car up to visit. Lantau is also known for its picturesque fishing village of Tai O. Villagers who live here build their homes on stilts to protect them against floods.

Lamma Island

This island is part of Hong Kong's New Territories and is known for its peaceful atmosphere. No cars or vehicles, apart from emergency vehicles, are allowed here. The only ways to get around are by foot or bike. Sham Wan beach on Lamma Island is an important breeding ground for sea turtles.

Central Plaza

Busy skies

Hundreds of airplanes zip through the sky above Hong Kong every day. Hong Kong International Airport was opened in 1998 in order to keep up with the increasing number of people flying in and out of this megacity. The airport was built on an artificial island, made by flattening two existing islands and raising the seabed between them. It has helped reduce noise and air pollution. Today, it is one of the busiest airports in the world with about 1,100 flights a day.

Hong Kong Convention and Exhibition Center

The Star Ferry carries passengers across Victoria Harbor, from Hong Kong Island to Kowloon.

RIVER ISLANDS

Islands are not only found in the ocean. They can also be found in rivers and lakes. River islands can be formed by sand or sediment building up in a certain part of a river. Or they can be made by erosion. The flow of a river can wear away the surrounding earth and rock, leaving a small island marooned in the middle of the water. Some river islands are small, whereas others stretch over hundreds of miles.

MANHATTAN
United States of America

Manhattan is one of the five boroughs in New York City. The island of Manhattan is famed for its towering skyscrapers, and the 102-story Empire State Building is one of the most recognizable high-rise buildings in the world. Manhattan is also an important commercial, financial, and cultural center of both the United States and the world.

ROOSEVELT ISLAND
United States of America

Roosevelt Island is a long, thin strip of land nestled in New York City's East River. Visitors can travel to the island by tram (an aerial cable car), subway, bus, or ferry. At the very southern tip of the island sits Franklin D. Roosevelt Four Freedoms Park, a memorial to Franklin D. Roosevelt, the 32nd president of the United States. The Park celebrates four important human rights—freedom of speech, freedom of worship, freedom from want, and freedom from fear.

MARAJÓ ISLAND
Brazil

Covering an area of around 15,482 square miles (40,100 km²), Marajó is one of the largest river islands in the world. The island is situated in an estuary where the Amazon River flows out into the ocean. It was formed over hundreds of years as the river flushed silt and other sediments out to sea. During the rainy season, when the water levels of the Amazon rise, about half of Marajó is flooded.

MAJULI
India

For many years, frequent river floods caused the island of Majuli in the Brahmaputra River to erode away. A local man, Jadav Payeng, noticed this and in 1979 began planting trees in order to revive the island. He knew that the trees would soak up water and prevent future floods. He single-handedly continued to plant trees on the island for the next 40 years, and the island is now a lush forest. Jadav Payeng has been nicknamed "the Forest Man of India."

ISLE OF SHEPPEY
United Kingdom

The Thames is the longest river in England and stretches for 215 miles (346 km). It has lots of aits, or river islands. From the year 835, Danish Vikings sailed up the Thames estuary and repeatedly raided one of these aits—the Isle of Sheppey in the county of Kent. The locals offered the Vikings payment, known as Danegeld, to make them go away and save the fertile farmland from being destroyed.

PRINCE EDWARD ISLAND
Canada

The emerald green farmlands, red clay roads, and beaches of Prince Edward Island provided the setting for the popular *Anne of Green Gables* books. The tales describe the life of a girl called Anne after she is adopted to help on a farm. The author's own experiences of growing up on this rural island are what inspired the books.

Faroe Islands

Isle of Sheppey
THE BRITISH ISLES
René-Levasseur
Mont Saint-Michel
Prince Edward Island
Île Sainte-Marguerite

Manhattan
NORTH ATLANTIC OCEAN
Gaiola Island

The Azores
THE BAHAMAS
Tenerife
CUBA

Turks and Caicos
Fadiouth

Marajó Island

SOUTH AMERICA

South Georgia

Deception Island
Danger Islands

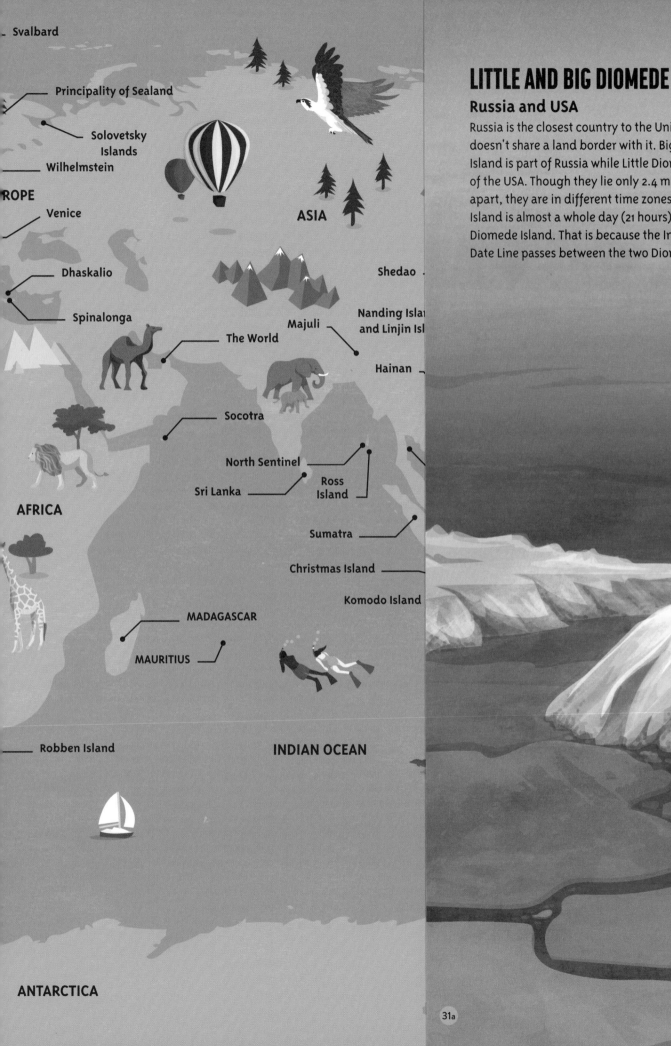

Svalbard

Principality of Sealand

Solovetsky Islands

Wilhelmstein

ROPE

Venice

ASIA

Dhaskalio

Spinalonga

The World

Shedao

Majuli

Nanding Isla
and Linjin Isl

Hainan

Socotra

North Sentinel

Sri Lanka

Ross Island

AFRICA

Sumatra

Christmas Island

Komodo Island

MADAGASCAR

MAURITIUS

Robben Island

INDIAN OCEAN

ANTARCTICA

LITTLE AND BIG DIOMEDE
Russia and USA

Russia is the closest country to the United States that doesn't share a land border with it. Big Diomede Island is part of Russia while Little Diomede is part of the USA. Though they lie only 2.4 miles (3.8 km) apart, they are in different time zones. Big Diomede Island is almost a whole day (21 hours) ahead of Little Diomede Island. That is because the International Date Line passes between the two Diomede Islands.

ARTIFICIAL ISLANDS

Islands form in many different ways. Some of them are naturally made and others are artificial, made by humans. Islands are built to create new land for homes or to keep noisy airplanes away from crowded cities. Others serve as an escape from the hustle and bustle of mainland life, or were created as a secret place to hide.

WILHELMSTEIN
Germany

In the 18th century, a German ruler called Count William ordered fishermen to create a tiny artificial island. They carried rocks in their boats and dropped them in the water to form a huge pile. The Count named the island Wilhelmstein and planned to use it as a fortress. Today, the island is a museum with ancient cannons, rifles, and maps on display.

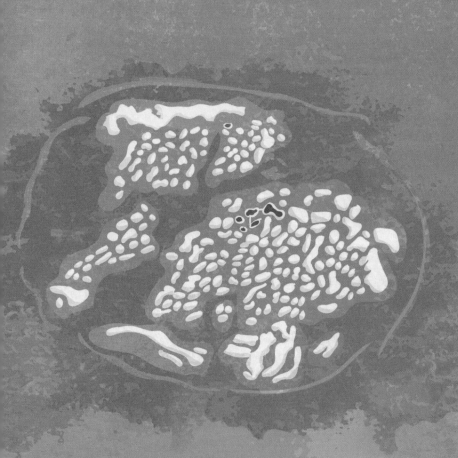

THE WORLD
United Arab Emirates

Not far from the city of Dubai lies an archipelago of 300 small islands built in the shape of a world map. They are made from sand that was dug up from Dubai's shallow coast, with the intention of creating a luxury holiday destination. There are buildings on only a few of the islands so far—the others remain uninhabited.

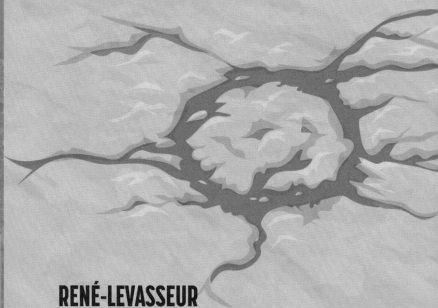

RENÉ-LEVASSEUR
Canada

This island began its life when a meteorite hit the area 214 million years ago and made a gigantic crater. In the 1960s, people flooded the crater, creating a lake and also the island. This island has a larger surface area than the lake surrounding it, and both can be clearly seen from space. They are nicknamed "the eye of Québec."

FLOATING ISLANDS
Peru

The indigenous Uros people collect totora reeds, which grow along the edges of Lake Titicaca. They then dry and bundle them to make floating islets. It is believed that they started this tradition so they could drift away and isolate themselves from the invading Inca people. For the Uros people, reed is an essential part of life. They use it to construct houses and boats, for food, and to weave containers and miniature models of rafts and hats to sell to tourists.

PRINCIPALITY OF SEALAND
North Sea

The British government built Fort Roughs Tower as a military fort during WWII. In 1967, army veteran Roy Bates moved there with his family and declared it an independent country called Sealand. They even issued passports. However, the United Nations didn't recognize Sealand as a country. Roy is no longer alive, but the island is looked after by a group of caretakers.

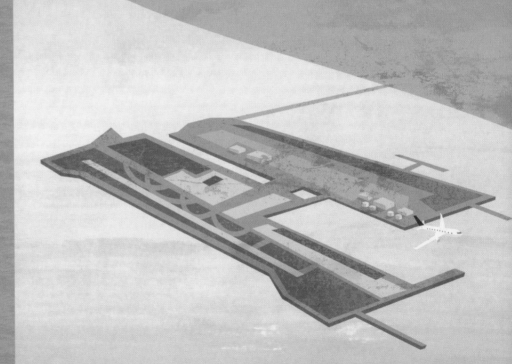

KANSAI INTERNATIONAL AIRPORT
Japan

The first airport to be built completely on an artificial island, Kansai serves the city of Osaka. Since it opened in 1994, the airport has been gradually sinking. Higher seawalls have been added around the island to block incoming waves and keep the airport dry. The main terminal rests on giant stilts that can be raised when the island floods.

SRI LANKA

Lying off the southern tip of India, the teardrop-shaped island of Sri Lanka is famed for its natural beauty and rolling hills draped in tea plantations. From the year 1815, Sri Lanka was known as Ceylon and was under British colonial rule. Sri Lanka became an independent country in 1948.

Sri Lanka is home to the Jaya Sri Maha Bodhi—the oldest living tree known to be planted by humans. It was planted in 288 BCE and has since been looked after by Buddhist monks and nuns. Statues, golden fences, and walls have been built around this sacred fig tree over the centuries to protect it from storms, monkeys, and bats.

The land of serendipity

Sometimes used loosely as a word to mean luck, the English word "serendipity" is derived from "Serendip," another ancient name of Sri Lanka. This tropical island is called the land of serendipity for a good reason: by chance, you might come across timeless ruins, an unspoiled beach, or a shy blue whale swimming to the ocean surface to gasp for breath.

Asian elephants

Sri Lanka has a large population of Asian elephants (around 4,000). Asian elephants are smaller than their African cousins and have smaller, curved ears.

Old, slow trains meander through endless hillsides of tea plantations and rustic villages.

Pilgrimage to the peak

This 7,359-foot (2,243-m-) tall mountain is known for the Sri Pada, or "sacred footprint." This is a rock formation, which followers of different religions believe is the footprint of their god or leader. Pilgrims climb 5,500 steps to reach the sacred Adam's Peak. The shrine at the summit brings together people from all religions practiced in Sri Lanka, from Buddhists and Hindus to Christians and Muslims.

Adam's Peak

Tasty tea

Almost 5 per cent of the Sri Lankan population works on tea plantations. Tea bushes are grown on mountain slopes, and the taste of the tea changes depending on how high the plants are grown. Workers pick tea buds by hand. They need to pick a lot to meet demand—tea is the second most consumed drink in the world after water. Around 7.9 pounds (3.6 kg) of fresh leaves are processed to get just two pounds (1 kg) of dried black tea.

A nod and a shake

In most cultures, people nod to say "yes" and shake their head side to side to say "no." But not in Sri Lanka. Here, people indicate "yes" or "okay" with a mixture of a head shake and a nod.

THE BRITISH ISLES

Situated off the coast of Europe, the British Isles are made up of Great Britain (England, Scotland, and Wales), Ireland, and a scattering of other, smaller islands. There are many different landscapes in the islands, ranging from mountains to rolling hills and farmland. The area is home to an array of wildlife and more than 71 million people.

1 ST KILDA
Scotland

The cliffs and sea stacks in this isolated archipelago are an important breeding ground for seabirds. Puffins come ashore in summer to lay their eggs in burrows, which they dig using their feet and bills.

2 SKYE
Scotland

This island was once home to dinosaurs, such as long-necked, plant-eating sauropods, similar to Brontosaurus. Visitors can still see their footprints preserved in the rock of the island.

3 ISLE OF MAN

The famous Isle of Man Tourist Trophy (TT) motorcycle race has taken place on this island since 1907. Contestants race on a 37.7 mile (60.73 km) circuit around the island's dangerous mountain course.

4 Giant's Causeway

Standing along the cliffs of Northern Ireland are around 40,000 column-shaped formations. Called the Giant's Causeway, the stone pillars are made of basalt rock.

5 Ben Nevis

The tallest mountain in the British Isles is Ben Nevis, which is in Scotland. Its summit reaches a towering height of 4,419 feet (1,347 m).

6 IRELAND

Often called the Emerald Isle, Ireland is known for its lush, green fields. Northern Ireland is part of the United Kingdom, but the Republic of Ireland is a separate country.

7 GREAT BRITAIN

This is the largest landmass in the British Isles. In it are England, Scotland, and Wales.

7

8 CALDEY ISLAND
Wales

This island's 40 residents have their own postage stamps and currency called the Dab, which was named after a local fish species. The island is also home to the Cistercian monks who live in Caldey Abbey.

9 LUNDY
England

Once home to Vikings and used as a port by pirates, Lundy is now a beautiful tourist destination. Atlantic grey seals can often be seen sunbathing on the rocks around the island. It is also a great place for stargazing, due to the lack of streetlights.

11 ISLES OF SCILLY
England

Only five of this collection of 140 or so islands are inhabited. Tresco Abbey Garden, on the island of Tresco, is home to more than 20,000 exotic plants, and Bishop Rock, although uninhabited, is the smallest islet in the world with a building on it—a lighthouse.

10

10 BROWNSEA
England

Famous for being the birthplace of the Scouts, Brownsea Island is where the first Scout camp took place. In 1907, Lord Baden-Powell and 20 boy scouts pitched their tents on the island and learned military skills.

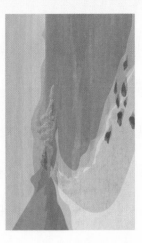

CHANNEL ISLANDS

This group of islands off the French coast of Normandy is famed for its beaches. Although English is the official language, a small number of people on the islands of Guernsey, Jersey, and Sark still speak dialects that have roots in Norman French.

SVALBARD

Norway

Svalbard is the northernmost inhabited group of islands in the world, located about halfway between Norway and the North Pole. There are nine main islands, but only Spitsbergen is permanently inhabited. Even though Svalbard is covered in ice, there is so little rain or snow that it is technically a desert.

These ice-capped islands are home to the largest land carnivores in the world: the magnificent polar bears. In order to find food, polar bears swim from ice sheet to ice sheet, stalking ringed and bearded seals. To take a break, the polar bears surface for air at a breathing hole or rest on the ice. Unfortunately, the ice sheets are getting smaller due to global warming, which means polar bears have to walk and swim farther in search of food.

Polar lights
On a dark and clear winter night, the northern lights will illuminate the sky.

Polar bear

Walrus

Whales, walruses, and seals all feed in these food-rich, icy waters.

Svalbard global seed vault
On Spitsbergen Island, a secure vault stores the world's most precious seeds. Built to withstand any disaster, it stores seeds for about 5,000 different plant species.

Seal

Underground cooking

Lake Furnas on São Miguel Island is home to a complex of geothermal springs. These contain hot water, which heats up inside the Earth and then rises to the surface. People have found an ingenious use for these springs and the surrounding warm earth—they use them to cook food. A traditional stew called *cozido* is made in a large pot and then buried underground to cook.

European bee-eater

Blue hydrangeas dot the landscape.

AZORES

Portugal

This archipelago of nine major islands and several islets stretches across more than 373 miles (600 km) of the North Atlantic Ocean. Each island is different from the next, but they all have volcanic origins. The last volcano to erupt was in 1957 off the coast of Faial Island.

The volcano (Mount Pico) on Pico Island is the highest point in all of Portugal, at 7,713 feet (2,351 m). These mountains are actually some of the tallest in the world if you measure them from their base at the bottom of the ocean to their peaks. The Azores are where three of the world's tectonic plates meet, so earthquakes are quite common.

MYSTERY ISLANDS

Islands are great places to find some of the most mysterious and curious phenomena on Earth. Humans don't always know why certain things are there, but that just adds to the fun of exploring our awe-inspiring world.

FADIOUTH
Senegal

While its origin is unclear, it is thought that local people harvested clams, scooped the meat out, and used the empty shells to build this tiny island. Even the cemetery, where both Christians and Muslims are buried, is covered in seashells.

EIL MALK
Palau

Imagine swimming in a massive swarm of golden jellyfish—don't worry, they don't sting! The jellyfish on Eil Malk live in a saltwater lake, in isolation from the ocean that surrounds the island. Some people think they were trapped in the lake 12,000 years ago when the sea level rose to the point where it began to fill the lake basin, but then dropped, leaving the lake isolated.

GAIOLA ISLAND
Italy

Since the 1800s, every owner of this villa set on two rocky islets has been plagued by disaster. There were accidents, murders, bankruptcy, and prison sentences. Finally, the locals decided the island was cursed, and nobody would live there. But in 2009, the owners of a villa opposite Gaiola Island were murdered. Is it a coincidence? Nobody knows for sure ...

SOLOVETSKY ISLANDS
Russia

Concentric swirls of shrub-covered stones form dozens of labyrinths on these islands. Archaeologists think they were created around the third century BCE, but have been unable to pin down their exact purpose. Some believe the labyrinths were used for ritual ceremonies. Others believe they may have symbolized a portal to the underworld for those who have died.

DHASKALIO
Greece

Archaeologists recently unearthed a 4,500-year-old monumental complex of buildings on this mountain-peak-shaped island. It features impressive stairways, drainage systems, and buildings made from marble. It is likely that the marble would have been brought in from nearby Naxos Island, and it would have taken at least 10,000 boat trips!

Dragon's blood tree

The dragon's blood tree is the symbol of Socotra. It is shaped like a giant opened umbrella and secretes a crimson resin from its trunk when it is sliced open. Its distinctive shape makes living in the arid desert possible. The dense tree canopy acts as a parasol, casting a cooling shadow on the ground. The shade stops any water from evaporating so that it can seep into the earth and be absorbed by the tree's roots.

Desert rose

Reaching the island by boat is dangerous as pirates are often found in the area.

Dragon's blood tree

SOCOTRA
Yemen

At first glance, the beautiful island of Socotra looks like a mysterious, barren planet. Its incredible landscape has a prehistoric feel, with rocks and ancient-looking trees covering the land. However, Socotra is actually full of life. It is called "the Galápagos of the Indian Ocean" because of the nearly 700 native species call it home.

Socotra was hit by three devastating cyclones in 2015 and 2018. Dozens of people were killed and thousands forced to leave their homes. It is feared that with climate change, tropical storms will become more frequent and isolated places such as Socotra will be at great risk.

Climbing snails

There are around 100 species of land snail on Socotra, of which 96 are found nowhere else on Earth. These snails often climb trees to escape the heat of the ground. But being up high exposes the snails to another danger— the hungry eyes of birds.

Pretty in pink

On Socotra the plants are specially adapted to their environment. The pink desert rose is a type of bottle tree that grows up to 16 feet (5 m) tall. It stores water in its trunk to survive the harsh climate.

Greedy goats

Sailors brought goats to Socotra a long time ago. There are now too many goats grazing in all parts of the island, eating sprouts and preventing trees from growing.

Word of mouth

Socotra is part of the country of Yemen, and Arabic is the official language. Older islanders also speak Soqotri, a language that is only spoken on two other islands and is in danger of dying out. Soqotri has no written form, so recordings of people speaking are the only way to document it. Poetry and song are part of everyday life and are important for keeping stories and culture alive.

VANISHING ISLANDS

Islands are affected by our changing Earth, from the ebb and flow of the tides to climate change. Some islands grow, while others shrink and can even disappear forever. They might be disappearing slowly, but in some places, people have already been forced to move away.

SANDY ISLAND

In 1774, Captain James Cook recorded an island he had seen in the Pacific Ocean. He called it Sandy Island. But when Australian scientists sailed in 2012, they found only open water. The "phantom island" could have just been a floating mass of pumice rock, not an island at all.

KIRIBATI

During the last century, at least eight islands in the Pacific Ocean have been swallowed by the rising sea. The islands of Kiribati are feared to be next. If this were to happen it would become the first country to be wiped off the map completely. Sea levels are rising because climate change is causing glaciers to melt. The 100,000 residents living on Kiribati's 33 coral islands might soon have no choice but to leave.

GREAT BLUE HOLE
Belize

The magnificence of this giant underwater sinkhole is best seen from above. However, scuba divers and snorkelers can also marvel at the way that the seabed drops away to what seems like nothingness. The Great Blue Hole is likely the remnant of a cave that was once on the Earth's surface, and it now sits inside an atoll called Lighthouse Reef. During the last ice age, the oceans began to rise, causing the cave to flood and collapse. Scientists have found stalactites, which are icicle-shaped pieces of rock made by dripping water, in this 407-foot- (124-m-) deep vertical cave.

KOH NANG YUAN
Thailand

This island is split into three small mounds connected by two strips of sand. When the tide is low, the sand serves as a walkway. But at high tide, the sand sinks into the ocean, and the only way to travel around the island is by boat. Many people enjoy jumping into the crystal-clear water to snorkel along the beautiful coral reefs that surround the island.

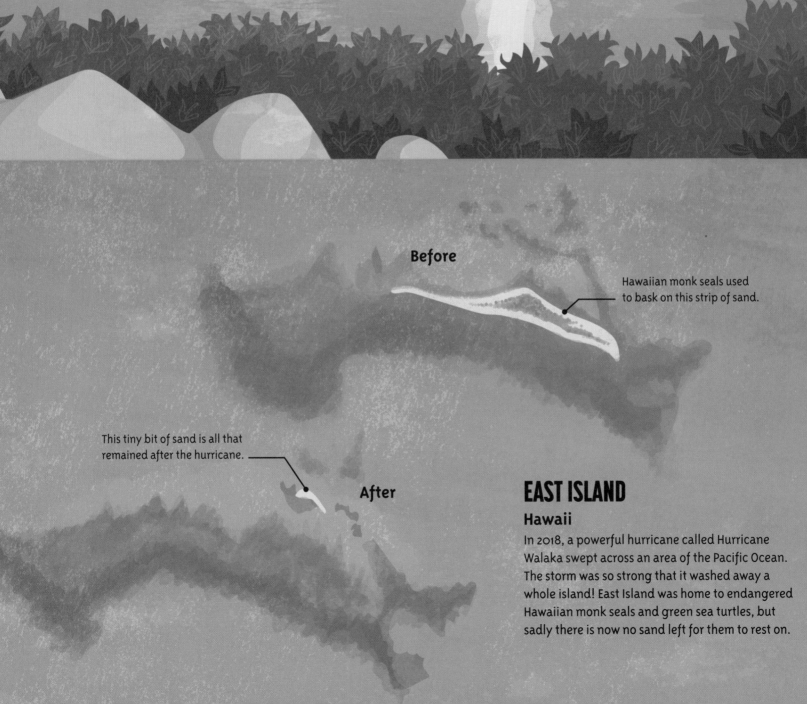

Before

Hawaiian monk seals used to bask on this strip of sand.

This tiny bit of sand is all that remained after the hurricane.

After

EAST ISLAND
Hawaii

In 2018, a powerful hurricane called Hurricane Walaka swept across an area of the Pacific Ocean. The storm was so strong that it washed away a whole island! East Island was home to endangered Hawaiian monk seals and green sea turtles, but sadly there is now no sand left for them to rest on.

LUCAYAN ARCHIPELAGO
West Indies

Thousands of breathtaking islands dot the Caribbean Sea. One particular archipelago, situated just north of Cuba, is well known for its beautiful sandy beaches, numerous coral reefs, and historical sites. But there is much more to discover on these Caribbean islands, from plants, to pirates and ... pigs!

The Lucayan Archipelago consists of the Commonwealth of the Bahamas and the Turks & Caicos Islands—a British Overseas Territory. There are more than 700 islands and cays. The main language spoken here is English.

THE BAHAMAS

The beaches of the Bahamas are covered with powdery sand and edged by calm, turquoise waters. They are often crowded with tourists who visit the beaches in droves. But what lies beneath the waves is even more spectacular: from dolphins and hammerhead sharks to sea turtles and parrot fish, these tropical reefs are full of life.

Pig beach

No humans live on the island of Big Major Cay, but many pigs do, and they love to swim. It is thought that they were left on the islands by sailors who wanted to come back and eat them at a later date. Many of the islands in the archipelago have the word "cay" in their names, which means a low island or reef.

Christopher Columbus

In his first voyage from Spain to the Americas in 1492, the explorer and colonizer Christopher Columbus stumbled upon land in the Bahamas. Many historians believe that the island he landed on first was Guanahani, which he later renamed San Salvador.

TURKS & CAICOS ISLANDS

Many people believe that the name "Turks" stems from the so-called Turk's head cactus, a local species whose red top resembles a fez hat worn by some Turkish men. Caicos comes from the term "cayo hico," which means "string of islands" in the Lucayan language.

Pirate hideout

Between 1690 and 1720, pirates used the cays around Turks and Caicos as hiding places. From there, they could attack passing Spanish galleons laden with treasures.

Gentle giants

Humpback whales visit the warm waters around Turks and Caicos every year to mate and give birth. The mothers stay there until their newborn calves are strong enough to make the long trip to the Arctic, where they feed on krill and small fish.

STRANGE SEA

The Lucayan Archipelago lies at the southern end of the Bermuda Triangle, a loosely defined region in the Atlantic Ocean. More than 50 ships and 20 airplanes are said to have mysteriously disappeared in the area. However, some scientists believe that there is really nothing strange about it. The large number of incidents could simply be due to human error, the weather, or the fact that lots of ships and planes travel through the area.

North America

Atlantic Ocean

GEOLOGICAL WONDERS

Islands are great places to see some of planet Earth's most spectacular, and often mind-boggling, geological formations. Some islands are the products of volcanic eruptions and others are the result of sinking land. These islands are remnants of Earth's long history and show the natural world at its breathtaking best.

MAURITIUS

Located in the Indian Ocean, Mauritius is a volcanic island that is surrounded by coral reefs. It was once home to the dodo, a now extinct, flightless bird. The sand and silt around an area of Mauritius' coast create an amazing optical illusion in the ocean. The sand appears to "fall" off the edge of an ocean shelf, making it look as though there is a waterfall under the water.

HUNGA TONGA-HUNGA HA'APAI

Tonga

This is one of Earth's youngest islands, created in 2014 after an underwater volcano sent a blast of steam and ash into the air. Initially, people thought it would take just a few months for the tuff (volcanic rock) to be washed away by the ocean. But the island kept growing. NASA scientists believe the island may hold clues to how water could have shaped a similar landscape on Mars billions of years ago.

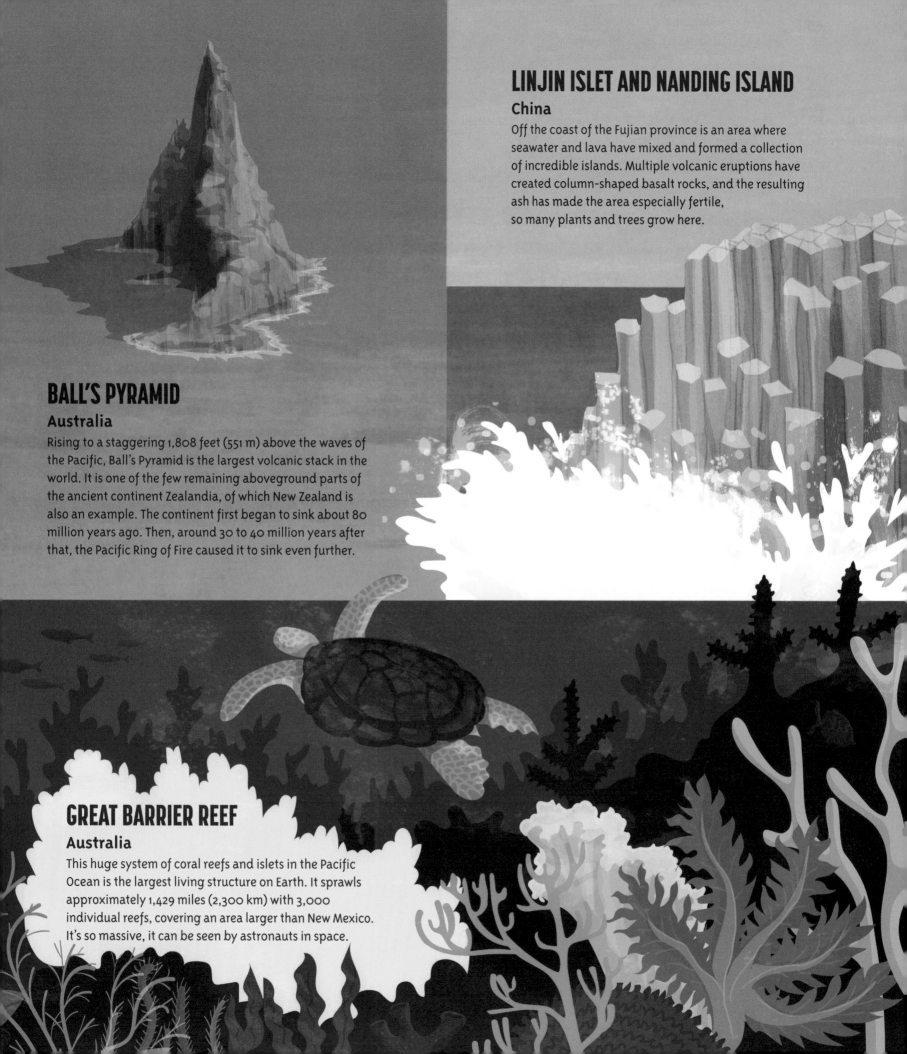

LINJIN ISLET AND NANDING ISLAND
China
Off the coast of the Fujian province is an area where seawater and lava have mixed and formed a collection of incredible islands. Multiple volcanic eruptions have created column-shaped basalt rocks, and the resulting ash has made the area especially fertile, so many plants and trees grow here.

BALL'S PYRAMID
Australia
Rising to a staggering 1,808 feet (551 m) above the waves of the Pacific, Ball's Pyramid is the largest volcanic stack in the world. It is one of the few remaining aboveground parts of the ancient continent Zealandia, of which New Zealand is also an example. The continent first began to sink about 80 million years ago. Then, around 30 to 40 million years after that, the Pacific Ring of Fire caused it to sink even further.

GREAT BARRIER REEF
Australia
This huge system of coral reefs and islets in the Pacific Ocean is the largest living structure on Earth. It sprawls approximately 1,429 miles (2,300 km) with 3,000 individual reefs, covering an area larger than New Mexico. It's so massive, it can be seen by astronauts in space.

VENICE

Italy

The city of Venice is built on 118 islands that are linked together by more than 400 bridges. There are no roads, just footpaths and canals. The sleek, black gondolas—traditional rowing boats—have been cruising around the narrow canals of Venice since the 11th century and today make for an iconic ride for tourists.

A tight squeeze

The narrowest street in Venice is called Calle Varisco and is only 21 inches (53 cm) wide. The city has many *calli* (alleys in Italian) like this one, but that has never posed a problem since people commonly travel by boat. That's also why the main entrance to most old houses faces the water.

Majestic masks

The annual Carnival of Venice happens in the lead up to the Christian celebration of Lent. It is famous because people dress up and wear extravagant, handcrafted masks. The origins of the masks go back centuries. While some Venetians used simple masks to hide their social status in the past, the "plague doctor" costume is perhaps the most bizarre and recognizable one. As a port city, Venice was hit by deadly plague outbreaks. Doctors wore masks with a curved beak like that of a bird and round eye holes covered with glass when tending to ill people. They often filled the beaks with aromatic herbs and plants in an attempt to avoid contracting the disease themselves.

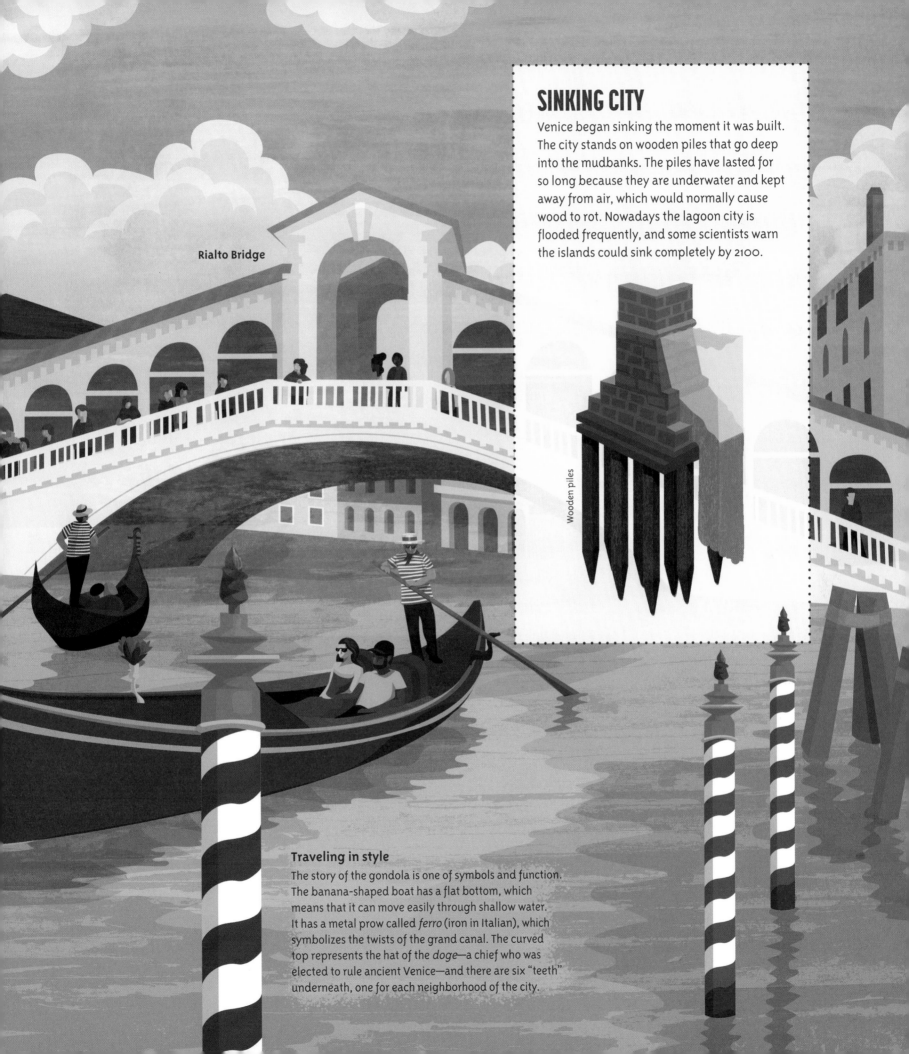

Rialto Bridge

SINKING CITY

Venice began sinking the moment it was built. The city stands on wooden piles that go deep into the mudbanks. The piles have lasted for so long because they are underwater and kept away from air, which would normally cause wood to rot. Nowadays the lagoon city is flooded frequently, and some scientists warn the islands could sink completely by 2100.

Wooden piles

Traveling in style

The story of the gondola is one of symbols and function. The banana-shaped boat has a flat bottom, which means that it can move easily through shallow water. It has a metal prow called *ferro* (iron in Italian), which symbolizes the twists of the grand canal. The curved top represents the hat of the *doge*—a chief who was elected to rule ancient Venice—and there are six "teeth" underneath, one for each neighborhood of the city.

FAROE ISLANDS
Denmark

Originally settled by seafaring Norsemen—the people who lived in medieval Scandinavia—the Faroe Islands are now part of the Kingdom of Denmark. However, this group of 18 islands has its own government and flag and has been self-ruling since 1948. The Faroe Islands produce their own electricity using windmills, tides, and waves. By 2030, the nation hopes to rely solely on electricity from renewable sources.

NO LAND IN SIGHT

The island group is pretty remote. It lies approximately 267 miles (430 km) southeast of Iceland, 373 miles (600 km) west of Norway and 186 miles (300 km) northwest of Scotland. Denmark, the country the Faroe Islands belong to, is more than 684 miles (1,100 km) away.

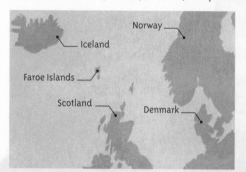

Norway

Iceland

Faroe Islands

Scotland

Denmark

Mulafossur
waterfall

Drangarnir rock

This set of two sea stacks—columns of rock in the sea, formed by wave erosion—is situated between the island of Vágar and the islet Tindhólmur. The strong waves have worn a hole straight through the middle of Stóri Drangur, or "Large Sea Stack."

Sub-sea tunnels

High-tech underwater tunnels connect the Faroe Islands together. The island of Vágar is connected to Streymoy, and Borðoy is connected to Eysturoy. This makes it easier for visitors to travel to and from the airport on Vágar.

In the Faroe Islands, no point on land is farther than three miles (5 km) from the ocean.

Green roofs

Many houses on the Faroe Islands have grass roofs. The grass acts as a great insulator in the winter and absorbs rainwater. Strips of waterproof birch tree bark are laid on the roof, and the grass is put on top to keep the bark in place. Once heavy with water, the grass compresses the log walls, stopping drafts from getting into the house. Instead of using lawnmowers, people rely on sheep to eat the grass on their roofs and keep it trim.

Sheep mapping

There are more sheep than people on the Faroe Islands—roughly 80,000 sheep compared with just 50,000 humans. In 2016, some residents used the sheep to persuade Google to include the archipelago in Street View, an online map. They strapped cameras to the backs of the sheep, and it was a great success!

Finding food

Most of the food on the Faroe Islands is locally sourced. Dried, fermented, and smoked fish and meats are often on the menu, along with whale meat and blubber. The climate is quite harsh and so only a few vegetables, such as potatoes, beetroot, carrots, and other root vegetables, can grow here.

Tea-planting past

The Fujian province is known for its history of tea planting. In the past, sailors transported the tea to Britain. They would race to be the first to arrive in London and secure the highest prices. In 1866, nine clippers assembled in the Min River for the famous Great Tea Race. A clipper is a fast sailing ship with a long, narrow hull and square-rigged sails. Taeping, a clipper carrying more than 490 tons (500 metric tonnes) of tea, took 99 days to sail to London. It docked just half an hour before its closest rival.

JIANGXIN PARK ISLAND

China

Amid the rugged mountains, cascading waterfalls, and meandering rivers of southeastern China lies the city of Fuzhou. Here, a number of aits are found along the Min River, but there is one exciting, green oasis that really stands out. Jiangxin Park Island—where no cars are allowed—is just a short walk over a suspension bridge. Riverside pavilions, grassy meadows, and a giant bookstore make it a pleasant place to spend a few hours. The island is full of greenery. Tall trees and flowering shrubs fill the air with a fruity scent. It is a wetland ecosystem, and many egrets and migratory birds enjoy this green haven as a stopping point on their journeys.

Staying connected

Sanxianzhou Bridge connects the mainland areas on either side of Jiangxin Park Island. It was built in 1996 and runs directly over the island, carrying cars over the Min River. The bridge has a single, 385-foot (117.5 m-) tall tower with multiple metal cables linking to either side of the roadway. The cable-stayed design helps distribute the weight of the bridge evenly and makes it more resistant to strong winds or earthquakes.

Shining bright
The traditional architecture on the nearby Zhongzhou Island is rather unusual for the region and a contrast to the modern skyscrapers in the background. The buildings are brightly lit at night.

Mouth of the river
At 359 miles (577 km) long, the Min River is the longest in Fujian province. Fuzhou sits on the lower end of the river, making it an important port city and entry point to the East China Sea.

New Year festivities
Jiangxin Park Island is not only a popular weekend destination for families. More than 20,000 visitors come to the island each year to celebrate the Spring Festival. This marks the beginning of the new year in the traditional Chinese calendar.

GLOSSARY

ARCHAEOLOGIST
Scientist who studies the buildings, tools, and other objects of people who lived in the past.

ARTIFICIAL
Something made by humans rather than occurring naturally.

BIODIVERSE
Habitat or region that has many different types of animals and plants.

BRITISH OVERSEAS TERRITORY
Area that is under the authority of the UK but does not form part of the UK itself.

CHARLES DARWIN
British scientist who studied nature. He is known for his theory of evolution by the process of natural selection, the idea that all species of life have evolved over time in response to changes in their environment.

CISTERCIAN MONKS
Monks who are members of the Roman Catholic religious order.

CLIMATE CHANGE
Process in which environmental conditions on Earth change over time. Today, these changes are mainly caused by an increasing level of carbon dioxide (CO_2) and methane (CH_4) in the atmosphere. Because our planet is warming, ice sheets are sinking, sea levels are rising and extreme weather events such as storms and floods are becoming more frequent.

COLONIALISM
Occurs when a country takes control of territory or people outside its own borders.

COMMONWEALTH
Group of 53 independent nations that were once associated with the British Empire.

CONSERVATION
Protection of certain things such as animals, plants, places or buildings.

CONTAGIOUS
When something, such as a disease, can spread from one person to another.

EARTHQUAKE
Vibrations in the ground produced by two large pieces of the Earth's crust suddenly moving past each other, or one underneath the other.

ENDEMIC
Plants or animals that are native to a certain place and not found anywhere else.

EQUATOR
Imaginary line running around the middle of the Earth at its widest point. The equator divides the globe into the northern and southern hemispheres.

EROSION
Gradual destruction or removal of rock or soil by weather, such as wind or rain, or by waves.

FERMENTED
Food or drink that has undergone a process in which the sugars have been changed into alcohol or acid. This happens because of a chemical process that involves yeast or bacteria.

FIESTA
Event marked by a celebration or party.

FORTRESS
Large, strong building that is protected from attack.

GALLEONS
Large sailing ships with several masts that were used by the Spanish between the 15th and 17th centuries.

GEOTHERMAL SPRINGS
Pools of hot water that have been heated naturally inside the Earth's crust.

IDEOLOGY
Set of opinions or beliefs shared by a group of people.

INDIGENOUS OR NATIVE
Person that originates from a particular place. The words also describe plants or animals that naturally exist in a place.

INTERNATIONAL DATE LINE
Imaginary line that runs from the north to the south pole, through the Pacific Ocean. It marks the boundary between time zones. If you were to cross the line from west to east you would go back one day. If you cross from east to west you would go forward one day.

MUTINEERS
People that rebel or refuse to obey authority.

NATURAL SELECTION
Charles Darwin's theory, which states that the animals or plants with traits that are most suited to their environment tend to survive, over those that are unsuited to their surroundings. The ones that survive are then able to pass along their genetic traits to their young. This process happens over a long period of time.

PRECIPITATION
Rain, snow, sleet or hail.

RENEWABLE SOURCES
Sources of energy that will not run out, for example sunlight and wind.

RING OF FIRE
Region along the Pacific Ocean that is home to over 450 volcanoes. Ninety per cent of Earth's earthquakes occur in this region.

SCANDAL
Action or event that is regarded as morally or legally wrong, causing general public outrage.

SEA STACKS
Steep columns of rock found in the sea near coasts. They are formed by wave and wind erosion.

SETTLEMENT
Place (often one that has been previously uninhabited) where people establish a community.

SPECIES
Group of living organisms that share characteristics and are capable of breeding and exchanging genes.

TECTONIC PLATES
Large, moving pieces of rock that make up Earth's outer layer. The movement of these plates can cause earthquakes and volcanic eruptions, while plates smashing together can form mountains.

UNITED KINGDOM
A country made up of England, Scotland, Wales and Northern Ireland.

VOLCANO
Opening in Earth's surface. When a volcano is active, it can let molten rock and gas from deep within the Earth reach the surface in sometimes violent and spectacular eruptions.

PRONUNCIATION GUIDE

Bajau (people)
badj-aow

Padre Island
pah-drey (Island)

Mont Saint-Michel
mon san mish-el

Roca Partida
roa-ka par-tee-da

Galápagos
gah-lah-pah-goss

Española
es-span-yo-lah

Fernandina
fur-nan-dee-na

Komodo Island
koh-moh-doh (Island)

Shedao
shed-aow

Aoshima
ah-oh-shee-ma

Madagascar
ma-da-gass-kur

Sumatra
soo-maah-truh

Fangataufa
fong-ah-too-fah

Mururoa
mur-rur-roh-ah

Hashima Island
hash-ee-mah (Island)

Netaji Subhash Chandra Bose Dweep Island
neh-tadj-ee soob-hash chan-draah bohs dweep (Island)

Shengshan Island
shuhng-shan (Island)

Île Sainte-Marguerite
eel sant-marr-guh-reet

Coiba
koy-buh

Robben Island
roh-bin (Island)

Alcatraz
al-kuh-traz

Spinalonga
spee-na-lon-ga

Luzon
loo-zon

Taal Volcano
tal vul-kay-no

Coron
koh-ron

Cebu
say-boo

Palawan
pu-laa-waan

Siquijor
see-kee-hor

Bohol
boh-hol

Siargao
shar-gaow

New Guinea
(New) gih-nee

Tenerife
ten-uh-reef

Hainan
hay-nan

Lantau Island
lang-daow (Island)

Marajó Island
ma-ra-djo (Island)

Majuli
muh-djuh-lee

Honshu
hon-shoo

Ellesmere Island
els-mir (Island)

Isola Tiberina
iz-oh-la tee-bur-ee-na

Suwarrow Atoll
suh-wah-roh at-ol

Toshima
toe-shee-ma

Pitcairn Island
pit-kairn (Island)

Foula
foo-luh

Nauru
nah-oo-roo

Hunga Tonga-Hunga Ha'apai
hung-gah tung-gah hung-gah hai-pay

Niijima
nee-jee-ma

Nishinoshima
ni-shee-no-shee-ma

Jadid and Sholan Islands
jah-did and show-lan (Islands)

Yaya Island
yah-yah (Island)

Zalzala Koh
zal-za-la ko

Uunartoq Qeqertaq
oo-oo-nar-tok ke-ker-tak

Norderoogsand
nord-er-rohgs-ant

Wilhelmstein
vil-helm-stighn

René-Levasseur
reh-nay-luh-vass-ur

Jaya Sri Maha Bodhi
jai-ya shree maha bod-ee

Isles of Scilly
igh-uhls ov si-lee

Lundy
lun-dee

Svalbard
sval-bar

Spitsbergen
spits-burg-un

São Miguel
saow mig-el

Fadiouth
fad-yoot

Eil Malk
eel mulk

Gaiola Island
gai-yo-la (Island)

Solovetsky Islands
suh-lov-et-skee (Islands)

Dhaskalio
das-kah-lee-oh

Kiribati
ki-ri-bah-tee

Koh Nang Yuan
ko nang yoo-wan

Hawaii
huh-wigh-yi

Lucayan Archipelago
loo-kyun ark-ee-pel-uh-go

Bahamas
buh-haah-muz

Caicos
kay-kohs

Mauritius
muh-rish-us

Linjin Islet and Nanding Island
lin-djin (Islet) and nan-ding (Island)

Faroe Islands
fair-oh (Islands)

Vágar
voh-ar

Tindhólmur
tind-hol-mur

Streymoy
stray-moy

Borðoy
bor-oy

Eysturoy
es-troy

Jiangxin Park Island
jyang-shin (Park Island)

Fuzhou
foo-jaow

Sanxianzhou Bridge
san-shyan-jaow (Bridge)

INDEX

SOURCES

Amos Carlos and Umgiesser George for The Conversation (2018). *Venice flooding is getting worse — and the city's grand plan won't save it.* https://theconversation.com/venice-flooding-is-getting-worse-and-the-citys-grand-plan-wont-save-it-106197

https://www.atlasobscura.com

https://www.bbc.com

Bonnett Alastair (2014). *Unruly places: Lost spaces, secret cities, and other inscrutable geographies.* Houghton Mifflin Harcourt.

https://www.smithsonianmag.com

https://www.britannica.com/place/Azores

British School of Athens (2019). *Evidence for advanced architectural planning at the early prehistoric site of Dhaskalio in the Aegean.* https://www.bsa.ac.uk/2019/05/06/evidence-for-advanced-architectural-planning-at-the-early-prehistoric-site-of-dhaskalio-in-the-aegean/

https://caldeyislandwales.com/

Cawley Charles (2015). *Colonies in conflict: The history of the British Overseas Territories.* Cambridge Scholars Publishing.

Cook islands. National Environment Service. *Suwarrow Atoll National Park.* https://environment.gov.ck/protected-areas/suwarrow-atoll-national-park/

Discover Hong Kong. *Central Plaza.* http://www.discoverhongkong.com/au/see-do/culture-heritage/modern-architecture/central-plaza.jsp

English Monarchs. *The Vikings.* http://www.englishmonarchs.co.uk/vikings_5.htm

Galápagos Conservancy. *Lonesome George.* https://www.galapagos.org/about_galapagos/about-galapagos/lonesome-george/

Gertner John for 360 Yale Environment (2019). *In Greenland's melting ice, a warning on hard climate choices.* https://e360.yale.edu/features/in-greenlands-melting-ice-a-warning-on-hard-climate-choices

Goldberg Walter M. (2017). *The geography, nature and history of the tropical pacific and its islands.* Springer.

Goudie Andrew S. and Viles Heather A. (2016) *Geomorphology in the Anthropocene.* Cambridge University Press.

Gholz Sophia (2019). *The boy who grew a forest: The true story of Jadav Payeng.* Sleeping Bear Press.

Gillespie Rosemary (2009). *Encyclopedia of islands.* University of California Press.

Guinness World Records. *Fastest Senior TT lap at the Isle of Man TT races.* https://www.guinnessworldrecords.com/world-records/fastest-lap-for-tt-senior-in-isle-of-man-tt-races/

Hacker Arthur (2012). *China illustrated: Western views of the middle kingdom.* Tuttle Publishing.

India Planning Commission (2008). *Andaman and Nicobar Islands, development report.* Academic Foundation.

Jackson Trevor A. 2002. *Caribbean geology: Into the third millennium: Transactions of the fifteenth Caribbean geological conference.* University of the West Indies Press.

Jennings Ken for CN Traveler (2017). *World's smallest inhabited island is about the size of a tennis court.* https://www.cntraveler.com/story/just-room-enough-worlds-smallest-inhabited-island

Kay James for Lonely Planet (2019). *This other Eden: the Azores, Europe's secret islands of adventure.* https://www.lonelyplanet.com/articles/this-other-eden-the-azores-europes-secret-islands-of-adventure

https://kids.kiddle.co

Kricher John C. (2006). *Galápagos: A Natural History.* Princeton University Press.

McLean Norman (2010). *Silent summer: The state of wildlife in Britain and Ireland.* Cambridge University Press.

Martin Laura C. (2011). *Tea: The drink that changed the world.* Tuttle Publishing.

Molloy Mark for The Telegraph (2018). *PG tips switches to plastic-free tea bags after 200,000 sign gardener's petition.* https://www.telegraph.co.uk/news/2018/02/28/pg-tips-switches-plastic-free-tea-bags-200000-sign-gardeners/

https://www.nasa.gov

https://www.nationalgeographic.org

National Trust. *Scouting and Guiding on Brownsea Island.* https://www.nationaltrust.org.uk/brownsea-island/features/scouting-and-guiding-on-brownsea-island

Nicholls Henry (2014). *The Galápagos.* Profile Books.

Norwegian Polar Institute. *Wildlife in polar regions.* https://www.npolar.no/en/species/

Principality of Sealand. https://www.sealandgov.org/

Rellie Annalisa and Hayne Tricia (2008). *Turks and Caicos.* Bradt Travel Guides.

Roza Greg (2009). *The creation of islands.* The Rosen Publishing Group.

Schalansky Judith (2014). *Pocket atlas of remote islands: Fifty islands I have not visited and never will.* Penguin Publishing Group.

Shetland Islands Council. *Shetland ponies.* https://www.shetland.org/things/explore-nature/shetland-ponies

Smith Oliver for The Telegraph (2017). *21 fascinating islands on the Thames you (probably) didn't know about.* https://www.telegraph.co.uk/travel/destinations/europe/united-kingdom/england/london/articles/fascinating-islands-on-the-thames/

Statistics Canada. *Census Profile. White Head Island* (2011). https://www12.statcan.gc.ca/census-recensement/2011/dp-pd/prof/details/page

Steinhuder Meer Tourismus. *Insel Wilhelmstein.* https://www.steinhuder-meer.de/meer-erleben/meer-kultur-erleben/wilhelmstein

Stevens Sidney for Mother Nature Network (2016). *10 new islands formed in the last 20 years.* https://www.mnn.com/earth-matters/wilderness-resources/stories/10-new-islands-formed-last-20-years

Structurae. *International database of galleries and gallery of structures. Sanxianzhou Bridge (Fuzhou).* https://structurae.net/en/structures/sanxianzhou-bridge

Tate Bria, Olivares Jose and Vogt Alfred for Google (n.a.). *Engineering Venice.* https://sites.google.com/site/engineeringvenice/

Turks and Caicos Tourism. http://turksandcaicostourism.com/about-turks-and-caicos/

U.S. Department of the Interior. National Park Service. *Little Brewster Island.* https://www.nps.gov/boha/learn/historyculture/facts-libr.htm

Villa on Dunbar Rock. https://www.dunbarrock.com/

Visit Faroe Islands. https://visitfaroeislands.com/

Whittacker Robert J., et al. (2007). *Island biogeography: Ecology, evolution, and conservation.* Oxford University Press.

https://www.worldatlas.com

World Population Review. *Kiribati population* (2019). http://worldpopulationreview.com/countries/kiribati-population/

What on Earth Books is an imprint of What on Earth Publishing
The Black Barn, Wickhurst Farm, Tonbridge, Kent TN11 8PS, United Kingdom
30 Ridge Road Unit B, Greenbelt, Maryland, 20770, United States

First published in the United States in 2020

Staff for this book: Editors, Katy Lennon and Ali Glossop; Art Director, Andy Forshaw;
Designer, Daisy Symes

Library of Congress Cataloging-in-Publication Data available upon request

ISBN: 978-1-9129201-6-7

Printed in Malaysia

10 9 8 7 6 5 4 3 2 1

whatonearthbooks.com